GREAT PEOPLE

MAHATMA GANDHI

Father of the Nation

written by **Anita Ganeri**
Illustrated by **Leighton Noyes**
and **Karen Radford**

hachette
INDIA

DIGBY is a treasure collector. Every Saturday he picks up a bargain at Mr Rummage's bric-a-brac stall and loves listening to the story behind his new 'find'.

HESTER is Digby's argumentative nine-year-old sister – and she doesn't believe a word that Mr Rummage says!

Mr RUMMAGE has a stall piled high with many curious objects – and he has a great story to tell about each and every one.

KENZO the barber has a wig or hairpiece for every dressing-up occasion, and is always happy to put his scissors to use!

Mrs BILGE pushes her dustcart around the marketplace, picking up litter. Trouble is, she's always throwing away the objects on Mr Rummage's stall...

Mr CLUMPMUGGER has an amazing collection of ancient maps, dusty books and old newspapers in his Rare Prints kiosk.

CHRISSY's Genuine Vintage Clothing stand has all the costumes Digby and Hester need to act out the characters in Mr Rummage's stories.

YOUSSEF has travelled far and wide and carries a bag full of souvenirs from his exciting journeys.

SAFFRON sells pots and pans, herbs, spices, oils, soaps and dyes from her exotic Spice Kitchen rigged up under a shady awning.

BUZZ is a street vendor with all the gossip. He sells sweets and pastries from a tray that's strapped to his back.

COLONEL KARBUNCLE sells military uniforms, medals, flags, swords, helmets, cannon balls, gas masks – all from the boot of his battered jeep.

PIXIE the fortune-teller sells incense, lotions and potions, candles, mandalas and crystals inside her exotic New Age tent.

PRU is a dreamer and Hester's best friend. She likes to tag along, especially when make-up and dressing up is involved.

JAKE is Digby's chum. He's got a lively imagination and is always up to mischief.

MR POLLOCK's toyshop is crammed with string puppets, rocking horses, model planes, wooden animals - and he makes them all himself!

5

Every Saturday morning, Knick-Knack Market comes to life. The street traders are there almost before the sun is up. And by the time you and I have got out of bed, the stalls are built, the boxes opened and all the goods carefully laid out on show.

Objects are piled high. Some are laid out on velvet: precious brooches and jewelled swords. Others stand upright at the back: large framed pictures of very important people, lamps made from tasselled satin, and old-fashioned washstands – the sort that drip when you pour the water in.

And then there are the things that stay in their boxes all day, waiting for the right customer to come along: war medals laid out in straight lines, stopwatches on leather straps and cutlery in polished silver for all those special occasions.

But Rummage's stall is different. Rummage of Knick-Knack Market has a stall piled high with a higgledy-piggledy jumble of things that no one could ever want. For who'd want to buy a stuffed mouse? Or a broken penknife? Or a pair of false teeth?

Well, Rummage has them all. And, as you can imagine, they don't cost a fortune.

Rummage's
"knick-knacks"

7

'What have I broken now?'

'Is something wrong?' asked Hester, looking sniffily at the jumble of objects on his stall.

'Hi, there, kids,' replied Rummage, blinking rapidly. 'I seem to have lost my specs. I can't see a thing without them and I keep knocking things off the stall.'

'Don't worry, Mr Rummage,' said Hester. 'We'll help you find…'

Digby Platt – seven-year-old collector of antiques – was off to see his friend Mr Rummage of Knick-Knack Market. It was Saturday and, as usual, Digby's weekly allowance was burning a hole in his pocket.

But Digby wasn't going to spend it on any old thing. It had to be something rare and interesting for his collection, something from Mr Rummage's incredible stall. Hester, his older sister, had come along too. She had secret doubts about the value of Mr Rummage's objects and felt, for some big-sisterly reason, that she had to stop her little brother from buying 'useless bits of junk'.

As Hester and Digby approached Mr Rummage's stall, they heard a loud CRAAASH!

'Oh bother,' said Rummage, crossly.

'Found them!' yelled Digby, holding up a battered pair of round, wire-framed spectacles he'd spotted on the counter.

'Found them!' yelled Mr Rummage at the same time, finding his spectacles on top of his head.

'So who do these spectacles belong to?' asked Digby, perching them on the end of his nose and peering into a mirror. 'Ooh, it's all gone blurry.'

'They belonged to a very great man called Mahatma Gandhi,' replied Rummage, smiling. 'And he probably found it hard to see from all the reading and looking at important documents he did.'

'And who, exactly, was Mahatma Gandhi?' asked Hester, suspiciously. She had a funny feeling that one of Mr Rummage's stories was about to begin.

'Mahatma Gandhi spent his life fighting for the rights of ordinary people in India,' declared Rummage. 'He helped to make India a free country.'

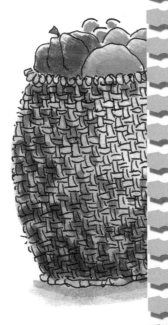

 # Mahatma Gandhi

Mohandas Karamchand Gandhi was born on 2 October 1869 in Porbandar, Gujarat. His parents Karamchand and Putlibai Gandhi had four children – three sons and a daughter – of whom Mohandas was the youngest. His family called him Mohania, a shortened version of his name. Later, he was given the name Mahatma which means 'great soul'.

Mahatma Gandhi became one of the greatest leaders India and the world has ever had. His mission was to free India from British rule without using violence. Through his own life and teachings, he helped to change the course of history in India and to influence people all over the world.

But let's find out more...

'Wow! Mr Gandhi must have been really amazing to do all that,' said Digby, admiringly.

'Oh yes, he was an extraordinary man,' said a soft voice from behind them. 'My grandparents told me all about him. I used to love listening to their stories about life in India.'

'Hi, Saffron,' said Hester. 'We did a project about India at school last term and it sounded like a really cool place. I'd love to go there and see all the tigers and peacocks, and ride on an elephant like a beautiful princess.'

'You've got a good imagination, Hester,' said Rummage, smiling. 'Just like Mahatma Gandhi, in fact. He liked listening to stories, but they filled his head with all sorts of pictures and ideas so that he couldn't sleep without a night light. Even as a teenager, a candle was always left burning by his bedside in case he got scared in the night.'

'Fancy being scared of the dark!' scoffed Digby.

'He was very shy when he was young,' said Saffron. 'As a teenager, he was smaller and thinner than his friends. And he was so worried that the others would poke fun at him,

he used to run all the way home after school.'

'Did his parents spoil him rotten because he was the youngest?' asked Hester, giving Digby a hard stare.

'He certainly got special treatment,' agreed Saffron, with a twinkle in her eye. 'That's often the way in many families. But it was probably his mother who spoiled him most. Mohania loved his mother dearly and she was devoted to her family. His father was much stricter and Mohania was a bit frightened of him.'

Family life

Mahatma Gandhi's father and mother

Family values

Mohandas's family were Hindus. They followed the ancient religion of Hinduism, which dates back at least 4,000 years. Most Hindus believe in a great spirit called Brahman, or God, and in hundreds of gods and goddesses who represent Brahman's many powers. Gandhi's mother was a devout Hindu. She never ate a meal without praying first to thank God for her food, and she visited the *mandir*, or temple, every day to worship. Mahatma Gandhi remembered her 'saintliness' and her 'deeply religious' nature all his life.

Goddess Durga

A place in society

Traditionally, Hindu society is divided into social groups called castes. Mohandas's family belonged to the *Vaishya* caste, which included merchants and businessmen. Far back in their family history, the Gandhis worked as grocers, but things had changed by the time Mohania was born. His grandfather, father and uncle all served as prime ministers to the Prince of Porbandar and other local rulers. This meant that the family was well respected in the local community and that they were reasonably well-to-do.

The Hindu god, Rama, whose name was the last word Mahatma Gandhi uttered

11

'But even though Mr Gandhi was shy, he still grew up to be a great freedom fighter? Isn't that right, Mr Rummage?' said Digby.

'It certainly is, Digby,' replied Rummage. 'One of the greatest there has ever been.'

'But who did he need to be free from?' asked Digby, looking puzzled.

'In his day,' Rummage continued, 'India was ruled by Britain. It all began when British merchants went to India to trade in valuable goods that they could sell for a profit back home. Gradually, their power grew and they turned from trading Indian goods to owning Indian land and, soon, India came under British rule. But Indians were often treated as second-class citizens in their own country. And there was very little they could do about it because the British made all the laws.'

'That was pretty unfair, wasn't it?' said Hester. 'No wonder that they wanted to be free.'

British India

East India Company

The English East India Company was set up in 1600 to trade with India and South-East Asia. At first, it traded only in spices but later added cotton, indigo, silk and other goods. The Company set up its first trading post at Surat, on the west coast of India, in 1612. By 1690, it had opened further posts in Calcutta (Kolkata) and Bombay (Mumbai). British traders were beginning to take over India.

The East India Company's army of Indian soldiers

Days of the Raj

As the East India Company's power grew, so did resentment among Indians. In 1857, this anger exploded into violence. The Company's army was largely made up of Indian soldiers called sepoys. They refused to use a new type of bullet in their guns due to religious reasons and mutinied. The rebellion spread quickly across northern India but eventually the British took control again. But the British government was horrified by what had happened and decided that the Company could not be trusted to run India any longer. So, in 1858, the Company was abolished and the British government took direct control of India. The British Raj, or 'rule', had begun.

British people came to India to work

A privileged life

From 1858, thousands of people arrived in India from Britain to work in the government, civil service and army. Many lived in luxury, compared to life back at home. In India, they could afford large estates in the countryside with teams of servants to look after their every need. While their husbands worked, the women painted, organized garden parties, and wrote letters home. For the men, polo and tiger-hunting were favourite hobbies. British and Indian people didn't really mix. Most British people were happy to rule India but that didn't mean that they had to get to know Indian people or their culture!

Jewel in the crown

Feast day for Edward VII's coronation as Indian Emperor

Indian Durbars

In 1876, Queen Victoria became Empress of India, although she never set foot in the country. A viceroy, or governor, represented the British Crown in India, with a Secretary of State for India in London. On 1 January 1877, a lavish ceremony called a durbar was held in Delhi to celebrate the event. Originally, durbars were held by Indian princes. Now they gave the British a chance to show off their power. It was a dazzling affair. Over 400 Indian princes attended and 15,000 soldiers took part in military parades. Until 1947, India was the 'brightest jewel' in the British crown'.

A steam locomotive on a mountain track

Indian railways

During the Raj, the British had thousands of kilometres of railway track laid across India. The railways were designed by British engineers and built by Indian labourers. The rail network helped the British to keep better control of the country. But it also allowed more Indians to travel. In the struggle for independence, many Indian leaders, including Mahatma Gandhi, took long train journeys across India to spread their message.

Taj Mahal

Among the many splendours of India, the Taj Mahal is famous all over the world. It was built by the Mughal emperor, Shah Jahan as a tomb for his beloved wife, Mumtaz. It took 20 years to complete and is built from white marble and was once decorated with precious stones, though these have long since disappeared.

The Hindu god, Rama

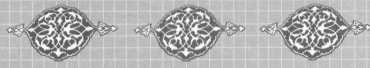

Princes and palaces

During the British Raj, about a third of India was made up of princedoms. These were ruled by princes who were allowed to keep their lands and titles, in exchange for showing loyalty to the British. Many of the princes lived in great luxury and were famous for their dazzling wealth. The Nizam of Hyderabad was said to be one of the world's richest men. His palace glittered with jewels, including pearls as big as marbles and egg-sized emeralds. In his home in the City Palace, Jaipur, it was said that the Maharaja of Jaipur had trouble getting to see his own treasure because it was so well guarded!

Amazing temples

There are thousands of temples all over India. Some are small roadside shrines; others are the size of small towns. One of the most splendid is the Ramanathaswamy Temple in Rameswaram in south India. Its magnificent hall is lined with carved pillars, and its main tower is over 50 metres tall. The temple is an important pilgrimage centre for Hindus. It is said that Lord Rama, one of the most popular Hindu gods, prayed to Lord Shiva here.

Growing up

An old painting of a Hindu wedding

Leaving home

In 1888, at the age of nineteen, Mohandas left his wife and family in India and sailed to Britain to study law. He wanted to study medicine, but his family preferred him to become a lawyer. His mother did not want Mohania to go, but he'd set his heart on it. In the end, his mother agreed on condition that he did not eat meat or drink alcohol. Like many Hindus, the Gandhis were vegetarians because they believed that it was wrong to harm or kill living things.

An early marriage

When Mohandas was 13 years old, his studies were halted by a very special event. He got married to Kasturbai Makanji, the daughter of a Porbandar merchant. His bride was also thirteen. Although the newly-weds spent much of their early married life apart, they came to love each other very much. They went on to have four sons – Harilal, Manilal, Ramdas and Devdas. After marriage, Kasturbai learned to read and write, and she was a clever and capable woman. Until her death in 1944, she stayed by Mahatma Gandhi's side through the long struggle for Indian freedom. Despite his happy marriage, he himself was strongly against child marriages, which he described as 'cruel'.

Wall hanging showing scenes from the Ramayana

'Mahatma Gandhi and his wife were very young when they got married, weren't they?' said Hester.

'Yes, they were,' said Saffron. 'But that was the custom at that time. And the children didn't really have a say. Their marriages were arranged by their families.'

'What does "arranged" mean?' asked Digby.

'Well, it means that parents chose a suitable boy or girl to marry their daughter or son,' continued Saffron. 'It might sound odd to you but it often worked very well. I mean, Mahatma Gandhi and his wife were happily married for 62 years!'

'Do people still get married so young?' asked Hester.

'No, they don't,' said Saffron. 'Today it's against the law. But parents still help their sons and daughters to find partners.'

'I saw a picture of a Hindu wedding in a book once,' said Hester. 'The bride was wearing a red sari. She looked very beautiful.'

'Yes, Hindu brides wear red because it's thought to be the colour of life,' said Saffron, smiling. 'They also wear lots of make-up and jewellery. And they paint patterns in henna on their hands and feet. It takes ages to get ready.'

'What's a wedding like?' asked Digby.

'Well, the main part of the ceremony takes place around a sacred fire,' said Saffron. 'The couple throw rice and barley into it as offerings to God. Later, they take seven rounds of the fire together. With each round, they make a promise to each other for a happy life ahead. The ceremony can last for about three hours, then there's a delicious feast.'

'Three hours!' exclaimed Hester. 'It must have been difficult for Mr Gandhi and his wife to sit still for so long! I don't think I could do it.'

'I bet they enjoyed the wedding feast afterwards!' said Digby.

'Mmm,' agreed Hester. 'I'm starving and it's not even lunchtime yet.'

'Well, what about trying some Indian sweets?' asked Saffron. 'I've brought some along for you to taste.'

'Oh yes, please,' said Digby, Hester and Rummage, all at once.

Saffron untied a ribbon and opened a box filled with brightly-coloured circles, squares and triangles, in pink, yellow and red.

'Wow!' said Digby, tucking into a sticky round yellow ball. 'Yummy!'

Hester wasn't so sure.

'It's a bit too sweet for me,' she said, nibbling at a silver-coated triangle.

'Yes,' said Saffron, grinning. 'Many Indians have got a very sweet tooth!'

'But people don't eat sweets every day, do they? We're not allowed to,' said Digby.

'No,' said Saffron. 'People give boxes of sweets as presents on special occasions such as weddings and festivals. Some people make the sweets themselves at home. Or you can buy them at stalls like mine.'

'I suppose it's like giving someone a box of chocolates for their birthday?,' said Digby, helping himself to a gooey green and yellow square.

'Just like that, Digby,' Saffron nodded. 'But the trick is not to eat too many of them in one go!'

Festival fun

There are hundreds of festivals throughout the year in India. Some celebrate events in the lives of the gods, goddesses, or holy people. Others mark particular times of the year, such as the arrival of spring. As a boy, Mohandas would have celebrated some of these festivals with his family. He might have joined his mother for a visit to the temple, and later there would have been special food, including sweets to eat.

A scene from the Ramayana

Colours and powders

Every February or March in India, the streets are filled with colour as people celebrate the festival of Holi. Holi traditionally marks the time of the spring harvest, but there are many legends attached to it. On the first night of Holi, people light bonfires to remember the wicked demoness Holika, after whom the festival is named. They say prayers and sing songs around the fire. Next day, the real fun begins. People splash each other with coloured water until their clothes are drenched in a rainbow of pink, red, yellow and blue.

Festival of lights

In October or November, Hindus everywhere celebrate the festival of Diwali. It marks the start of the New Year for many Hindus and is a time when they also remember the story of the god Rama, and his wife Sita. This is a story which Mohandas would have heard many times in his childhood. It is told in the Ramayana, one of the most sacred Hindu texts, and tells how Rama was born a royal prince but was cheated out of his kingdom by his step-mother who sent Rama and Sita into exile in the forest. There, Sita was kidnapped by Ravana, the evil demon-king of Lanka. With the help of the monkey general, Hanuman, Rama rescued Sita and returned to claim his throne. To guide Rama and Sita home, Hindus light small clay lamps, called *diyas*.

'So what happened to Mohandas once he reached London, Mr Rummage?' asked Digby.

'Well,' said Rummage, eagerly taking up the story again. 'It must have been a terrible shock! He had never been away from home before. He still found it difficult to speak English and he was just as shy as ever.'

'Do you think he was homesick?' wondered Hester. 'I think I would be.'

'I expect so,' replied Rummage. 'A few months before he left India, his wife had a baby son and he must have missed them both very much. But it didn't stop him trying his best to fit into English society.'

'How did he do that?' said Digby.

'For a start, he tried to dress like a fashionable Englishman. In the daytime, he wore a striped silk shirt with a colourful tie, striped trousers and a double-breasted waistcoat. On top, he wore a morning coat and a silk top hat. Then he put on leather gloves and shoes, and carried a silver-topped cane. In the evening, he'd change into a dark evening suit.'

'He must have looked very smart,' said Hester.

'Oh yes,' said Rummage. 'He took great care of his appearance. He spent ten minutes every morning just combing and brushing his hair.'

'Perhaps that's going a bit far,' said Hester, whose hair was always a bit of a mess.

'What else did he do, Mr Rummage?' asked Digby.

'Well, he took speech lessons to try to improve his English. And he also took dancing and violin lessons, but he wasn't very good at them and soon gave up!'

Life in London

Even though Mohandas wanted to fit into English society, he didn't forget the promises he had made to his mother. So he didn't drink alcohol or eat meat, even though his English friends tried to persuade him to. He soon found a vegetarian restaurant not far from where he was studying and became a member of the Vegetarian Society of England. He also learned how to cook. To save money, he made his own breakfast of porridge and cocoa, then went to the restaurant for lunch. Dinner was bread and cocoa at home. Later, he learned how to make carrot soup.

Spiritual guide

While he was in London, Gandhi read the Bhagavad Gita, one of the most sacred Hindu texts. Its message is the importance of doing your duty without thought of any reward for yourself, and it was to become Mahatma Gandhi's daily guide throughout his life.

The Indian coastal town of Porbandar in the early 1900s, Mahatma Gandhi's birthplace

Becoming a lawyer

Mohandas enrolled at the Inner Temple, one of four law colleges in London. He gives very few details about his student days in his autobiography. We know that he learned French, Latin, physics and law, but not much more than that. In June 1891, he passed his final exams and became a lawyer.

A London street in the early 1900s

'Did Mr Gandhi stay and get a job in London?' asked Hester.

'No, he didn't,' replied Rummage, smiling. 'As soon as he'd finished his studies, he got straight on a boat and sailed back home to India.'

'I bet his family were glad to see him,' said Digby.

'Oh yes, they were,' said Rummage. 'But they also had some sad news to tell him – his mother had died while he was away. His family had kept the news from him because they knew how much he loved his mother and didn't want him to cut short his studies to come home.'

'That's terrible,' said Hester, sadly. 'But at least he had his wife and son to cheer him up.'

'Yes, but he also needed to find a job, and quickly, to support his family,' continued Rummage. 'His brother helped him to get work as a lawyer, but he was a hopeless failure! At one court case, he was struck by such bad stage fright that he couldn't say a word!'

'I wish Hester would get stage fright,' muttered Digby under his breath. 'Then we'd all have some peace and quiet.'

'Anyway,' continued Rummage, before Hester could answer back. 'Things didn't look good for Mohandas...

He had no job, no money and another baby on the way. Then his luck changed. A firm in Porbandar offered to send him to South Africa for a year as their lawyer. Of course, he snapped up the offer and in April 1893, he left his wife and family again and sailed off to start a new life. He was gone for 21 years.'

Mohandas in South Africa

When Mohandas arrived in the British and Dutch colony of South Africa, he found that the Indian community was treated very badly by white people. Before long, he experienced this for himself. Despite having a first-class ticket, he was thrown off a train because Indians were not allowed to travel first class in case they offended the white passengers.

The Indian Ambulance Corps, founded by Mahatma Gandhi

Indian Ambulance Corps

When war broke out in 1899, Mohandas told Indians that, as British subjects, they should support the British war effort. But he didn't believe in violence, so he organized over 1,000 Indian volunteers into the Indian Ambulance Corps. He hoped that their bravery would help their struggle for equal rights. But things didn't work out as planned.

In 1899, war broke out between the British and Dutch states of South Africa

Indian Congress

Many Indians had come to South Africa to work as labourers. They were paid very badly and had very few basic rights. Mohandas realized that something had to be done to improve their lives. So he enouraged local Indians to organize themselves. In 1894, he helped to form the Natal Indian Congress to campaign for equal and just treatment for Indians.

Peaceful protests

When the government ordered every Indian to carry a special pass, Mohandas led a protest against the unfair law, using peaceful means. He called this peaceful protest 'Satyagraha', which means truth-force. He believed that the best way to change an unjust law was to break it deliberately but without using violence. It worked! In 1914, the government agreed to recognize the basic rights of Indians. Feeling his job was done, Mohandas decided to go home.

'So, did Mr Gandhi carry on with his "sat-what's-its-name" when he got back to India?' asked Digby.

'Satyagraha,' laughed Rummage. 'And yes, he did but not straight away. His friends knew about his campaigning in South Africa and wanted him to get involved in Indian politics. But he'd been away for over 20 years and he wasn't very well known in India. I suppose he also felt he'd lost touch with what India was like.'

'So how did he find out more about his country?' asked Hester.

'Well, a close friend advised him to travel around India for a year with "his ears open and his mouth shut". That way, he could see what India was like for himself. Gandhi took his friend's advice and travelled all over India by train.'

'I hope he didn't get thrown off this time!' said Digby.

'No, he didn't!' said Rummage. 'He was able to visit cities, towns and villages. But he was shocked by the poor conditions in which many people lived, especially in the countryside.'

'That's terrible,' said Hester. 'What did he do about it?'

'Well, he realized that, before he could tackle the big problem of freedom for India, he had to look at local problems first,' said Rummage. 'He also decided that it would be better for him and his family if they, too, lived a simple life like the ordinary people of India.'

A simple life

Mahatma Gandhi settled at Sabarmati near the city of Ahmedabad in Gujarat. There he set up the Satyagraha Ashram community where his family and followers could live and work together. They lived a simple life, growing their own food, spinning cloth, and studying and praying together. Mahatma Gandhi believed that the way people behaved was much more important than possessions. He continued to work on his ideas on Satyagraha, or peaceful protest, which he'd begun in South Africa. His followers became known as Satyagrahis, or 'people who seek the truth'.

To set a good example, Gandhi spent several hours a day at his spinning wheel

Food and fasting

Like many Hindus, Mahatma Gandhi was a vegetarian for most of his life. As a boy, he had once eaten goat's meat in secret with a school friend. But the meat made him sick and he'd felt so guilty he'd dreamt the goat was bleating in his stomach! So he now lived on a very simple diet of nuts, seeds, fruits and goat's milk. He often fasted, or went without food for several days. He believed that this cleansed his body and mind.

 ## Spinning skills

Mahatma Gandhi decided to give up his suits and ties, and dressed in a plain white cotton loincloth and sandals – the clothes of a humble Indian villager. He believed that India needed to stop using western goods and rely on the goods it made itself. This was the way to win independence. So he encouraged people to spin their own cotton and make their own clothes with hand-spun *khadi*. To him, spinning wasn't just a useful thing to do – it was also a political statement.

'On his tour of India, Mahatma Gandhi met a man called Rabindranath Tagore,' said Rummage, taking up the story again.

'Who was he?' asked Digby. 'Was he a lawyer like Mr Gandhi?'

'No, Tagore was a famous poet and writer, who helped to make Indian writing better know in the West. The two men became great friends. In fact, it was Tagore who gave him the name "Mahatma".'

'What does "Mahatma" mean?'

'It means "great soul",' said Rummage. 'Tagore saw that his friend was a very gentle and peaceful person. So he gave him a remarkable name. And it stuck with him for the rest of his life.'

'What else was special about Mr Gandhi?' asked Digby.

'Well,' said Rummage. 'For a start, he always practised what he preached. He believed in treating all religions with respect. And last but not least, he was always on the side of people who were poor or unfairly treated, like the people called untouchables, for instance.'

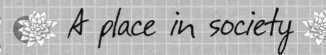

A place in society

The caste system

Traditionally, Hindu society is divided into groups, called castes, based on the jobs people did. Hindus believe that everyone is born into one of these castes. The top caste is that of the Brahmins, or priests. Next come the Kshatriyas, or rulers and soldiers, and after them, the Vaishyas, or traders and farmers. The fourth caste is the Shudras, or ordinary labourers. Mahatma Gandhi's family belonged to the Vaishya caste. When he decided to go to England, some members of his caste were furious. They warned him that, if he went abroad, he would stop being a Hindu. He went anyway. Luckily, for Indian travellers today, the caste rules are much more relaxed!

An Indian mendicant

Indian society was divided both by caste and class

The untouchables

A fifth group of people were considered to be outside the caste system because they did the dirtiest jobs, such as street cleaning. These people were called untouchables. Untouchables weren't allowed to touch higher-caste Hindus or anything they touched. Untouchables were also forbidden to enter Hindu temples, homes and shops. This meant that they were forced to live apart from other people, often in squalid quarters, in the worst conditions.

Children of God

Mahatma Gandhi called the caste system 'a hideous system'. And throughout his life, he stood up for the untouchables. He welcomed a family of untouchables into his community, even though this upset many people. He believed that untouchables had the same rights as everyone else and should be treated with dignity and respect. He even began to clean the communal toilets himself, a job traditionally done by untouchables. He did this to show people that there was no shame in it. He renamed the untouchables 'Harijans' which means 'Children of God'. Today, they prefer to be called Dalits which means 'stepped on' or 'oppressed'.

'Everyone in India must have heard of Mr Gandhi by now,' said Hester.

'Yes, most people knew the Mahatma,' agreed Rummage. 'But he probably wasn't the sort of leader they'd expected to have.'

'What do you mean?' asked Digby.

'I mean that Mahatma Gandhi didn't look much like a freedom fighter,' said Rummage. 'He wasn't tall or strong-looking, and he didn't have a powerful voice for making speeches. He was a small, slight figure and was so soft-spoken that it was sometimes difficult to hear what he said.'

'And he wore thick glasses,' added Digby, looking at the spectacles he was holding in his hand.

'I'm not surprised, with all the books he had to read,' said Hester.

'Indeed,' said Rummage. 'He was always reading or writing. He wrote hundreds of letters to friends. And his fame spread far and wide. Many people came to ask for his help. One of them was a poor farmer from Champaran in north-east India. He told Mahatma Gandhi that he and his fellow farmers had to set aside part of their land to grow indigo, a plant used to make blue dye, for their British landlords. Then the landlords took all the profits for themselves.'

'That doesn't seem fair,' said Digby. 'After all, the farmers did all the hard work.'

'That's exactly what Mahatma Gandhi thought,' replied Rummage. 'He visited the farmers and found out more about their troubles. Then he reported the problem to the British government.'

'Did they do anything to help the farmers?' asked Hester.

'Yes, they agreed to let the farmers keep a quarter of the profits,' Rummage said.

'It wasn't as much as Mahatma Gandhi wanted, but it was better than nothing.'

Struggle for freedom

On strike!

Gandhi's work for the indigo farmers showed he was no longer prepared to let the British order him about in his own country. He thought it was wrong that Indians had so few rights and freedoms, when more than half a million Indians had bravely fought with the British Army during World War I. So he called on Indians to go on strike and spend the day praying and fasting instead. The strike was a great success and India ground to a halt. But it also led to violence and he immediately called off the campaign.

Massacre in Amritsar

After the violence of the strike, public meetings were banned in some Indian cities. But in Amritsar, in Punjab, a short distance from the Golden Temple, 20,000 protestors gathered in Jallianwalla Bagh, a ground surrounded by walls. A British officer arrived with his troops to stop the meeting. Without any warning, he ordered his men to open fire on the crowd. Nearly 1,000 Indians were killed and more than 1,500 wounded. Horrified by the bloodshed, Indians realized that they'd have to fight even harder for their freedom.

The Golden Temple in Amritsar

Campaign for home rule

In 1920, Mahatma Gandhi campaigned for Indians to run their own country. He asked Indians to refuse to buy British goods, stop using British-run services, and refuse to pay their taxes. Thousands of people followed his call. Some gave up well-paid jobs with the British. Many more burned their British-made clothes and goods on bonfires. The British were furious. In 1922, he was arrested and sentenced to six years in prison. He was released two years later when he fell ill with appendicitis.

The Salt March

By 1928, some Indians were getting impatient. They felt that Gandhi's non-violent tactics weren't getting results quickly enough. So Gandhi warned the British that he would lead another protest unless India was given dominion status by 1 January 1930 – this meant India would be free but still be part of the British Empire. The British Government turned down his request, leaving Mahatma Gandhi no choice. So, this time, he demanded full independence for India. Nothing less would do. The whole of India waited to see what he would do next...

Under the Salt Laws of 1882, only the British Government was allowed to make and sell salt. Everyone from every strata of society needed salt. The salt tax was a great burden on the poorer people and yet they had no choice but to pay. And salt gave him the idea he'd been waiting for. On 12 March 1930, he and 78 volunteers set out from Sabarmati to march to the town of Dandi on the shores of the Indian Ocean. There, he planned to break the law by taking his own salt from the sea. It was a journey of 368 km along winding dirt roads. The marchers covered about 20 kilometres a day and reached Dandi on 5 April. Huge crowds lined up to watch them pass by and hundreds joined in. Early on the morning of 6 April, he went down to the seashore, picked up a piece of salt and, in doing so, broke the law.

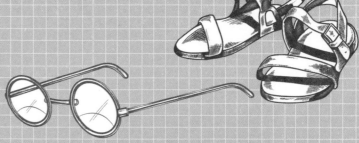

The result of this simple act was astonishing. All along the coast, people began making and selling their own salt. Soon, much of India had joined in the non-violent protest. By the end of the year, Mahatma Gandhi and thousands of others were in prison. But the campaign had worked brilliantly. The British agreed that people living near the sea could make salt for their own use, and released all the demonstrators. In return, Mahatma Gandhi called off the campaign.

'It seems like Mr Gandhi's freedom fighting was really taking off,' said Digby. 'Well, freedom "not-fighting", I suppose you'd say.'

'Indeed,' said Rummage. 'And by now he was seen as the real leader of India.'

'So the British had to take him seriously!' said Hester.

'That's right,'said Rummage. 'In fact, they even invited him and other Indian leaders to a conference in London to talk about India's future.'

'Did he go?' asked Digby.

'He certainly did,' replied Rummage. 'And everywhere he went, he was given a warm welcome. You see, the Salt March had been reported all over the world so everyone knew who he was. And he was very friendly with everyone he met.'

'I bet he didn't have any time for sight-seeing, though?'said Hester.

'Well,' said Rummage. 'He did go to Buckingham Palace and have tea with the King and Queen! But hang on a tick – somewhere I've got an old newspaper with some photos of him in it. It's a bit faded but I think you'll be interested in it. Ah yes, here it is, under this pile of old hats.'

'Oh, look,' said Hester, peering at the newspaper. 'Mr Gandhi's wearing his Indian clothes and sandals. He must have been freezing. He hasn't even got a coat!'

'Sadly, though, the conference was a failure,' Rummage continued. 'It seemed the British had no plans to set India free. So he went back to India and guess what happened to him there?'

'I bet Mr Gandhi was sent back to prison again!' sighed Digby.

'You're quite right,' said Rummage.

'Despite being in prison, Mahatma Gandhi continued his work,' Rummage went on. 'And in 1935, the British Government finally agreed to give Indians a greater say in running their country.'

'Did that mean India was free now?' asked Hester.

'Not yet, Hester,' said Rummage. 'It was a start but many Indian demands still hadn't been met. Matters came to a head during World War II.'

'It lasted from 1939 to 1945,' said Digby, proudly. 'We did it in history.'

'Show-off!' hissed Hester.

'Exactly, Digby,' smiled Rummage. 'Well, millions of Indian troops fought in the war for Britain. In return, the British promised that India would be free.'

'Did the British keep their promise?'

'I'm afraid not,' said Rummage, frowning. 'So, in 1942, Mahatma Gandhi launched a movement called the "Quit India" movement. He told the British that they must leave India or face another non-violent campaign. But the British didn't listen. Instead, they threw Mahatma Gandhi and the other Congress Party leaders back into jail. But even that didn't stop riots and protests breaking out all over India.'

'I bet he was upset about that,' said Digby.

'He was,' continued Rummage. 'Mahatma Gandhi hated violence, as you know. But he had other things on his mind. His wife, Ba – that was his nickname for her – was sent to prison with him. But she became very ill. She died in his arms just three months before he was released.'

'Oh no,' said Hester and Digby, softly.

'He missed her terribly. After all, they'd been married for 62 years,' said Rummage. 'He couldn't imagine life without her by his side.'

Independence at last!

Religious hatred

During the 1940s, trouble between India's two main religions - Hinduism and Islam - began to tear the country apart. Many Muslims were afraid that Hindus would take control when India became independent. Eventually, Muslims wanted a part of India all to themselves. They even had a name for it - Pakistan. Mahatma Gandhi was horrified. He believed that Hindus and Muslims should live together peacefully. In August 1946, Muslims protested on the streets of Calcutta (Kolkata). It was a bloodbath. In three days of violence, thousands of Hindus and Muslims were killed. Mahatma's teachings on non-violence were being ignored.

Independence

With the violence growing out of control, the British Government reached a decision. They would give India independence, and divide it into Hindu India and Muslim Pakistan. On the stroke of midnight on 14-15 August 1947, India became a free country. A cheering crowd watched as Prime Minister Nehru raised the new saffron, white and green Indian flag. But one person was missing from the celebrations...

India divided

Mahatma Gandhi didn't take part in the celebrations. Instead, he spent the day fasting and praying for peace. Freedom had come for India, but at a terrible price. It had been impossible to divide India neatly into Hindu and Muslim parts. So, the states of Punjab in the west and Bengal in the east had been divided along religious lines. The Muslim parts of these states formed West and East Pakistan. And they lay on opposite sides of India. Millions of people suddenly found themselves stranded in the 'wrong' country. As they tried to escape over the new borders, Hindus and Muslims turned against each other. About 14 million people became refugees. Mahatma Gandhi felt that he'd failed in his life's work. He announced that he was ready to fast to death to stop the violence in Delhi. A few days later there was peace.

Gandhi's death

Just after 5 pm, on Friday 30 January 1948, Mahatma Gandhi left Birla House, the huge mansion he was staying at in Delhi. Leaning on his followers for support, Mahatma Gandhi walked into the garden for his evening prayer meeting. About 500 people were waiting for him. Among them was a man called Nathuram Godse. A fanatical Hindu, Godse blamed Mahatma Gandhi for favouring Muslims and looked on him as an enemy of the Hindu faith. As Mahatma Gandhi passed by, Godse stood up and bowed to him. Then he took a pistol from his pocket and fired three shots at Mahatma Gandhi. As the Mahatma slumped to the ground, his spectacles fell to the floor. 'Hey Ram,' he murmured.

Funeral procession

The next morning, Mahatma Gandhi's body was carried to the banks of the Yamuna River. A million and a half people marched through Delhi, following the funeral procession, while crowds watched from the roadside. Three aircraft flew overhead, showering the crowds with rose petals. By the river, Mahatma Gandhi's body was placed on a funeral pyre made of sandalwood. According to Hindu custom, it was to be burned to ashes. At 4.45 pm, his son, Ramdas, lit the fire and the mourners began chanting prayers. When the fire finally went out, his ashes were collected. They were later taken by train to be scattered in India's holiest rivers.

For a while, the stall was strangely silent. Even Hester was solemn and quiet.

'What a sad ending to the story,' she said, eventually.

'Yes,' said Saffron. 'My grandparents told me that everyone in India was so shocked and stunned, no one could believe that Mahatma Gandhi was dead. They said that people were crying in the streets. No one knew what to do.'

'I'll always treasure these spectacles,' said Digby. 'And I'll always remember Mahatma Gandhi whenever I put them on.'

'Oops!' he added, as he bumped into Rummage's stall.

'You'd better be careful,' said Rummage. 'I'm always losing my spectacles and I wouldn't want you to lose those. Mahatma Gandhi is one of my heroes. He was one of the most peaceful men of his time and yet he became one of the most inspiring leaders the world has ever seen.'

'It's all right, Mr Rummage,' said Hester, holding on to Digby's arm. 'I'll make sure he looks after them. 'And I'll try to do it in a non-violent way so that Mr Gandhi would approve!'

'I'm very glad to hear it!' said Rummage, standing up and knocking over an old vase.

'Now where have I put my spectacles? I had them a minute ago.'

'THEY'RE ON TOP OF YOUR HEAD!' shouted Hester, Digby and Saffron, hooting with laughter.

'Oh, so they are!' chuckled Rummage. 'What would I do without you? Now then, it seems I've got another customer. So goodbye, both of you. I'll see you next Saturday for another story.'

'Bye, Mr Rummage! Bye, Saffron,' said Digby. 'I really liked the sweets!'

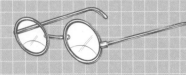 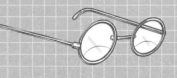
Mohandas Karamchand Gandhi was born at a time when his country was under British rule. It seemed impossible that a small, slender man in a loincloth and sandals could take on the might of the British Empire.

From his early days in South Africa, Mohandas championed the cause of people who were poor and downtrodden. These included the Indian workers in South Africa and the untouchables back home in India. He himself thought of everyone as equal, regardless of the colour of their skin, or their religion. One of his greatest qualities was to inspire others by his example. He always practised what he preached, even if this meant regular trips to jail. His curious mind picked up ideas from many different traditions. Together, these were shaped into his belief in Satyagraha, or non-violent protest. And it became a very powerful weapon in the fight for Indian Independence. Most remarkably, at a time of two terrible world wars, Mahatma Gandhi showed that peace could bring about extraordinary results.

But the Mahatma was no ordinary man. Through his philosophy of peace and non-violent action, he helped to set his country free and influenced millions of people – not only in India but around the world.

Many people took up Gandhi's message of peaceful protest. They included Martin Luther King, Jr. (1929-1968), the leader of the civil rights movement in the USA. Although the two men never met, King used Satyagraha as a key part of the struggle to end racial hatred and get equal rights for black people. He and his fellow campaigners staged sit-ins, boycotted buses and held marches, just as Mahatma Gandhi had done. Even though King was assassinated in 1968, aged just 39, his use of non-violent protests had already done much to change US laws and to bring hope to black people everywhere.